P9-EER-567

Nuclear Energy

by Jim Ollhoff

VISIT US AT

WWW.ABDOPUBLISHING.COM

Published by ABDO Publishing Company, 8000 West 78th Street, Suite 310, Edina, MN 55439. Copyright ©2010 by Abdo Consulting Group, Inc. International copyrights reserved in all countries. No part of this book may be reproduced in any form without written permission from the publisher. ABDO & Daughters™ is a trademark and logo of ABDO Publishing Company.

Printed in the United States of America, North Mankato, Minnesota
112009
012010

 PRINTED ON RECYCLED PAPER

Editor: John Hamilton
Graphic Design: John Hamilton
Cover Photos: Jupiter Images, iStockphoto
Interior Photo: Corbis, p. 15, 17; Getty Images, p. 11,19, 20, 21, 28; iStockphoto, p. 1, 5, 10, 24, 29; Photo Researchers, p. 6, 7, 8, 9, 13, 18, 22, 23, 25, 27; U.S. Dept. of Energy, p. 14.

Library of Congress Cataloging-in-Publication Data

Ollhoff, Jim.
  Nuclear energy / Jim Ollhoff.
    p. cm. -- (Future energy)
  Includes index.
  ISBN 978-1-60453-936-3
  1. Nuclear engineering--Juvenile literature. 2. Nuclear engergy--Juvenile literature. 3. Nuclear power plants--Juvenile literature. I. Title.
  TK9148.O45 2010
  333.792'4--dc22
                        2009029853

Contents

Nuclear Energy

Facing page: A nuclear power plant at night. The large cooling tower is ejecting a plume of steam. Some say nuclear energy is the answer to the problem of burning fossil fuels, which puts too much carbon dioxide into the air and contributes to global warming. Others worry that a nuclear accident could pollute the land for centuries.

Nuclear energy produces electricity through a process called fission. In 1956, the first commercial nuclear power plant opened in England. In the United States, as of 2008, there were 104 nuclear reactors producing about 20 percent of the country's electricity needs.

Nuclear energy doesn't produce greenhouse gasses, and no pollution is released into the air. Compared to coal or other fossil fuels, the emissions from nuclear power plants are very clean. Some people say we should build more nuclear power plants to reduce greenhouse gas pollution. However, the waste from nuclear energy stays dangerously radioactive for thousands of years.

Another kind of nuclear energy is called fusion. This is the energy that powers the sun and the stars. However, scientists cannot yet control the process on earth. If scientists could learn how to create and control fusion, it could become an energy source that is clean and would never run out. Many people hope that fusion will be the energy of the future.

How Does Fission Work?

Facing page:
Computer artwork of atomic fission.
Right: A neutron (blue) collides with a uranium-235 nucleus (grey). The neutron combines with the nucleus to form uranium-236. This is a highly unstable element the undergoes nuclear fission (splitting), which produces a vast amount of energy, plus the elements barium-141, krypton-92, and three neutrons.

Everything is made up of tiny atoms. Atoms are made up of protons, neutrons, and electrons. Some elements, like helium, are small, composed of only one proton. Some atoms are large. Uranium, the heaviest element in nature, has 92 protons.

Because uranium is so heavy, the atoms break apart easily. This is why uranium is used as a fuel in nuclear reactors. Fission happens when a neutron crashes into a uranium atom and splits it. The neutrons from that atom then crash into other atoms, and so on. When huge numbers of neutrons are crashing into atoms, it is called a chain reaction. A chain reaction produces heat.

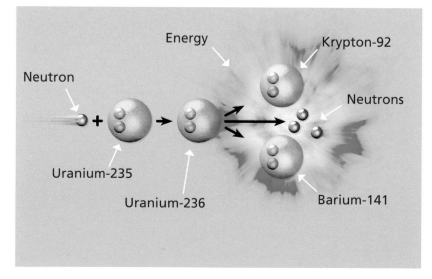

Energy

Krypton-92

Neutron

Neutrons

Uranium-235

Uranium-236

Barium-141

At the center of a nuclear power plant is the reactor, where fission takes place. Inside the reactor is a supply of uranium, called the core. If the uranium reactor were left on its own, the chain reaction would get out of control. It would become so hot that the reactor would melt, and then it would pass right through the floor. Dangerous radiation would escape into the air. This would be a terrible disaster, called a meltdown.

Scientists have a way to keep the uranium from getting too hot. This is accomplished with cooling rods, or control rods, that are lowered into the nuclear reactor. This keeps the reactor from getting too hot, and controls the chain reaction. If more heat is needed, they can pull some of the cooling rods up and out of the reactor (although they would never pull all of them completely out of the reactor). If they needed to cool the reactor a little, they can put more cooling rods into the reactor.

Below right: A boiling water nuclear reactor. The core (yellow columns) is suspended in water (blue). Heat made by the nuclear reaction boils water into steam (red). This turns a turbine (green), which drives an electricity generator (grey). The steam then passes through a condenser, which uses water from a cooling pond (lower right), before being passed back into the reactor chamber. Control rods (blue, between core columns) can be raised or lowered to control the reaction.

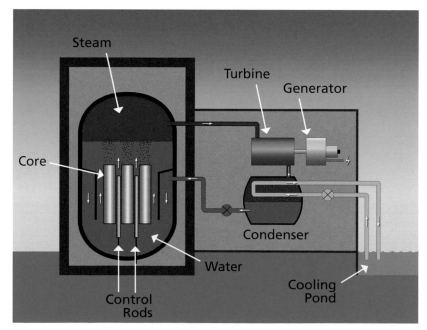

So, how does a nuclear power plant produce electricity? A nuclear power plant controls the chain reaction of uranium to produce heat in the reactor. Water is pumped through the hot reactor. The water heats up and turns into steam, and the hot steam turns turbines. Then, a generator converts the motion of the turbines into electricity.

Uranium is used for fuel in power plants. It is a non-renewable energy source, but it is fairly common. Much of the uranium used in North America is mined in the Western states.

Uranium itself is radioactive. Radioactivity is a stream of particles or rays given off by certain kinds of matter. Radiation can cause serious illness or death. The uranium is kept in a sealed building called a containment building. Radiation does not get into the water or air unless there is an accident or disaster.

Below: Fuel rods being lowered into the French Chooz B1 nuclear power station's reactor core. The reactor itself is immersed beneath the blue water, and lifting machinery is being used to raise and lower the fuel rods (center) into the core (circular area). There are 205 fuel rods used in this reactor core.

Advantages of Nuclear Energy

Facing page: The Exelon Byron Nuclear Generating Station in Byron, Illinois.

Below: A nuclear power plant cannot create a thermonuclear explosion.

Most of the energy in North America currently comes from fossil fuels—coal, oil, and natural gas. Burning these fuels produces greenhouse gasses, such as carbon dioxide. Most scientists believe that carbon dioxide traps the sun's heat, which increases the temperature of the earth.

As climate change has become more of a concern in recent years, some people have begun to promote nuclear power. Nuclear energy produces no greenhouse gasses. Steam is the only gas that is released into the atmosphere by nuclear plants.

Another advantage of nuclear energy is that it is such a powerful source of energy, more than fossil fuels. From a relatively small amount of nuclear fuel, a very large amount of energy is produced.

Some people mistakenly think that if something goes wrong in a nuclear power plant, there will be a giant nuclear explosion. This is not true. Nuclear power plants can't become thermonuclear bombs.

Disdvantages of Nuclear Energy

Facing page: A worker in a nuclear power plant uses remotely controlled handling arms to manipulate high-level radioactive waste sealed in thick, double-walled, lead-lined concrete units. He is protected by three feet (.9 m) of leaded glass, and security badges that monitor the level of exposure.

Perhaps the biggest problem with nuclear energy is the waste it produces. The fuel in nuclear reactors eventually gets used up, leaving a waste product. This waste is highly radioactive, and it remains radioactive for 10,000 years or more. So far, there is no good way to make it safe.

Spent nuclear fuel must be stored somewhere. But where do you store something that stays deadly for thousands of years? That's the problem.

People have suggested that all of the waste should be stored in a central location somewhere. The waste could be mixed with concrete or glass, and then sealed in barrels. But what if the barrels got rusty and corroded? What if rainwater leaked into the storage area and got contaminated? What if there was an earthquake that damaged the barrels? What if terrorists broke into the storage facility and stole some of the waste? Many people think there should be a central storage facility, but no one wants the waste storage facility near them.

It is difficult to find a place that is water-free, earthquake-free, and can be secured and protected for thousands of years. Beginning in the late 1980s, Yucca Mountain in Nevada was explored as a possible storage site. It was planned to be deep underground, with barrels stored in a maze of tunnels that were cut out of the rock. For about 20 years, tests were conducted to prove if Yucca Mountain would be a good storage site. However, uncertainty about water seepage, the discovery of an earthquake fault under the mountain, and the opposition of Nevada residents killed the project. So, for now, most nuclear waste is stored in casks on the grounds of nuclear power plants.

Below: A curved tunnel inside the Yucca Mountain nuclear waste repository.

Before the 1970s, people thought that nuclear waste could be reprocessed and used again for fuel. But reprocessing creates a byproduct called plutonium. This material can be used to make nuclear weapons. In the 1970s, President Jimmy Carter discontinued civilian reprocessing because of the danger of weapons-grade nuclear material increasing in availability.

Keeping nuclear power plants safe from terrorists is a concern. The biggest danger is that terrorists could get in and damage the reactor or the waste containers, which could release radioactivity into the air. Nuclear power plants have highly trained security and police SWAT teams that protect the facilities.

Below: An armed security officer stands guard at the Diablo Canyon Nuclear Power Plant in California.

Three Mile Island

Two famous accidents at nuclear power plants drastically changed the direction of nuclear energy. One of these was at a nuclear power plant called Three Mile Island, near Middletown, Pennsylvania.

On March 28, 1979, a technical problem occurred in a water pump at Three Mile Island. The water was cooling the reactor. When the pump failed, the reactor began to overheat. Another technical failure occurred in a valve that was releasing excess steam. The operators of the plant didn't have enough information to figure out what the problem was, and they made a number of errors that made the problem worse.

During the tense next few days, engineers tried to cool the reactor and solve the other problems that were happening inside the plant. The governor of Pennsylvania advised children and pregnant women, the most vulnerable to radioactivity, to leave the area. Radioactivity was released into the air, and almost half of the reactor melted down. However, the reactor meltdown was contained and eventually cooled. Although no one died in the accident, it made people fearful of the nuclear industry.

Facing page: The top portion of a nuclear reactor at Three Mile Island on the day the accident occurred. The partial core meltdown did not result in any deaths, but a significant amount of radioactivity was released into the environment.

Nuclear Disaster: Chernobyl

Facing page:
The destroyed
Reactor Four of the
Chernobyl nuclear
power plant.
Below: Chernobyl's
radioactive plume
several days later.

The 1979 accident at Three Mile Island created a lot of fear. However, a few years later, a much bigger disaster occurred in Eastern Europe. In the country that is now Ukraine, there was a nuclear power plant near the city of Chernobyl. Ukraine used to be part of a collection of states called the Soviet Union.

On April 26, 1986, Soviet engineers conducted a safety experiment on the nuclear reactor. The experiment called for the reactor to be reduced to 50 percent power. But the engineers made a mistake in their calculations, and the power dropped too far. When the reactor power got too low, it began to release hydrogen gas as a waste product. The engineers then tried to fix the problem by raising the reactor's power too quickly, and the reactor overheated.

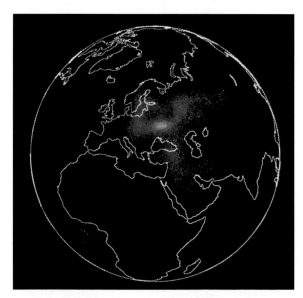

An explosion blew the top off the containment building, exposing the reactor. Massive amounts of radioactivity were released into the air. At first, the Soviet government was slow to act, and it tried to cover up the accident. However, as winds carried radioactive particles northwest, it became difficult to hide the disaster. Radiation alarms were triggered as far away as Sweden, and later even in Canada.

Months later, the Soviet government reported that 31 people had died from immediate exposure, including power plant technicians and rescue workers. The reactor was hastily covered in concrete to prevent further radiation from leaking.

Nearby cities such as Pripyat were evacuated. They remain ghost towns even today. Large areas of Ukraine and Belarus are off-limits to people, and will continue to pose a radiation threat for hundreds of years, perhaps even thousands of years. People are not supposed to live in the contaminated areas, but some do anyway.

Below: A hastily abandoned classroom in the ghost town of Prypyat, which lies close to the Chernobyl nuclear site. All 45,000 residents of the city were forced to flee their homes after the disaster.

It is unknown how many people died as a result of radiation sickness in the months and years after the Chernobyl accident. The Soviet government was very secretive, and sometimes did not keep records. Further, many people contracted cancer, but it is impossible to say how many got cancer from the radiation, and how many would have contracted the disease anyway. Some estimates say that 1,000 people died of radiation-related diseases. Other estimates say 100,000 or more were killed.

After the Chernobyl and Three Mile Island accidents, it would be almost 20 years before another nuclear power plant was approved for construction in the United States.

Below: Five-year-old Anya Petrushkova stands behind 4-year-old Andrey Sabirov, who rests his head on the side of his hospital bed. Both children were diagnosed with cancer after the Chernobyl disaster.

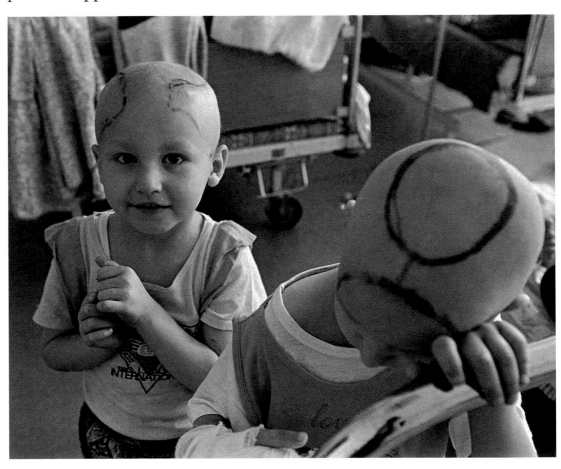

What is Fusion Energy?

Fission energy breaks up large molecules of uranium. Fusion energy, however, combines very small molecules. One type of fusion takes two hydrogen atoms, the smallest in nature, and fuses them together. Two hydrogen atoms fused together create helium plus a large amount of energy. Fusion is the process that powers the sun and the stars, giving us heat and light.

Positively charged atoms naturally combine with negatively charged atoms, but positive-positive and negative-negative combinations are hard to achieve.

Below: A cross-section of the sun. Fusion is the solar process that gives off heat and light.

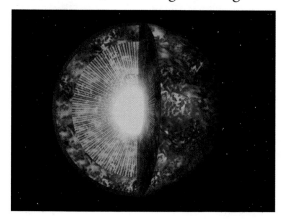

The nucleus of a hydrogen atom has a positive charge, so getting hydrogen atoms to fuse together is very difficult. Extremely high temperatures—millions of degrees— are needed to make atoms fuse. If the heat could be held in a small space, the energy could continue to create fusion.

In stars, gravity holds the heat in a confined space so that fusion continues to happen.

But how do scientists create that much heat on earth? Scientists haven't done it yet, but one possibility is to use a magnetic field strong enough to hold the heat and the fusion reaction together. Very powerful lasers could create enough heat for the fusion to occur. Scientists are trying to find ways to create and sustain a fusion reaction. They hope to have success within the next few decades.

Below: A nuclear fusion reaction. Tritium and deuterium (upper left & right) nuclei collide to form helium (lower left) and a neutron (lower right).

Fusion: The Hope and the Reality

Scientists have been trying to make fusion power for 50 years. While knowledge has constantly advanced, it's unclear if the technological hurdles will be overcome anytime soon.

It takes a lot of energy to make a process hot enough for fusion. However, if it works, fusion will produce more energy than is required to make it. Scientists believe that fusion will have no waste products—no greenhouse gasses or long-term radioactive waste.

Below: Could nuclear fusion someday provide us with an energy source that is both limitless and safe?

Scientists also believe that fusion power plants will be safer than fission power plants. With fusion, there is little chance of anything melting down or releasing radiation. While fusion reactors would still be radioactive, most scientists believe that the reactor elements would only be radioactive for 50 to 100 years. The radioactive elements from fission reactors, on the other hand, will stay radioactive for thousands of years.

So far, scientists have been able to create a fusion reaction, but have not been able to sustain it. It has not yet produced more energy than it consumes. Research continues into all the aspects of fusion research. If fusion works, it could be the best energy source of the future. However, it's still too early to say if fusion will ever work.

Below: A diagram of an experimental nuclear fusion reactor that scientists hope is working by 2016.

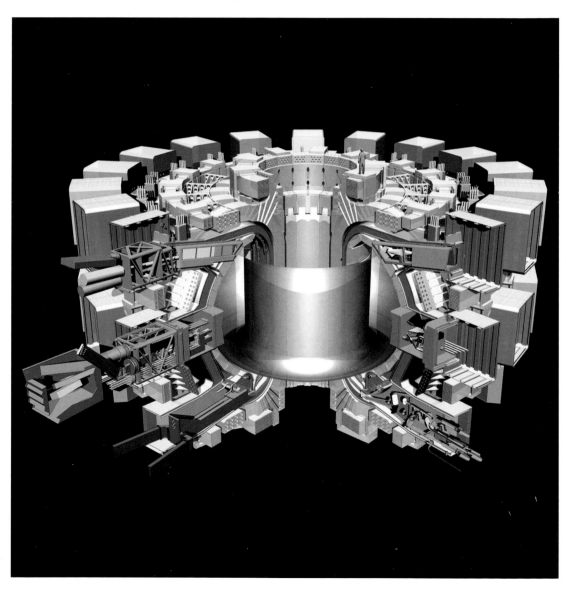

The Future of Nuclear Energy

After the accidents at Three Mile Island and Chernobyl, no nuclear power plants were built in the United States for a long time. In the early 2000s, permits began to be issued for the building of nuclear power plants. However, the power plants were much more expensive to build than originally planned. A number of construction projects have stopped, leaving the future of these power plants uncertain.

Some say that new technology will ensure that nuclear power is safer than in the 1970s and 1980s. But critics say that no technology is ever perfect, and the risk of a nuclear accident is too great.

With the abandoning of the Yucca Mountain facility in Nevada to store toxic nuclear waste, more questions remain. Where will nuclear waste be stored? Currently, there are no plans to store the radioactive waste for the long term.

Facing page: The future of nuclear energy is in our hands. It could be a source of limitless power, but many tough questions have yet to be answered.

Many of today's nuclear plants are getting old, and will need to be closed soon. The expense of building new nuclear plants is high. Supporters say we need nuclear power to limit greenhouse gasses. Critics of nuclear energy say that solar and wind power can meet our electricity needs. The debate continues on the risks and benefits of nuclear power.

In early 2009, there were more than 400 nuclear power plants worldwide. About 40 new nuclear power plants are under construction. Currently, almost 20 percent of the energy in the United States is supplied by nuclear power. Will high costs prevent additional nuclear power plants from being built? Will the risks of nuclear waste kill the industry? Or, in a world that has a warming climate, will nuclear energy become more popular, since it emits no greenhouse gasses?

Below: Workers at the construction site of a new nuclear power plant in Flamanville, France.

Instead of fission, will fusion become the energy of the future? Will the technological hurdles be overcome, making fusion the perfect energy source? Or will fusion power have unforeseen problems?

These questions are still being discussed today, and answers are hard to find. Only time will tell whether fission or fusion—or neither—will become the energy of the future.

Below: A nuclear power plant in Lower Saxony, Germany.

Glossary

CARBON DIOXIDE

Normally a gas, carbon dioxide is a chemical compound made up of one carbon atom and two oxygen atoms. Its chemical symbol is CO_2. Carbon dioxide in the earth's atmosphere acts as a greenhouse gas.

CHAIN REACTION

When the collision of atoms creates a fission reaction, which creates more collisions and reactions.

CONTAINMENT BUILDING

The part of a nuclear power plant that contains the nuclear reactor. The building protects the reactor and keeps the radioactivity from getting into the environment.

CONTROL RODS

Rods that are lowered into a nuclear reactor to cool the reactor and slow the chain reaction.

FISSION

The splitting apart of atoms. In nuclear power plants, uranium atoms are split.

FOSSIL FUEL

Fuels that are created by the remains of ancient plants and animals that were buried and then subjected to millions of years of heat, pressure, and bacteria. Oil and coal are the most common fossil fuels burned to create electricity.

Natural gas is also a fossil fuel. Burning fossil fuels releases carbon dioxide into the atmosphere, contributing to global warming.

FUSION

When atoms are fused together. In the sun, atoms of hydrogen are pushed together to form helium.

GREENHOUSE EFFECT

The earth naturally warms because of the greenhouse effect. The surface of the earth absorbs some solar radiation, and reflects some. The reflected rays either pass back into space, or are absorbed and reflected back by gasses in the earth's atmosphere. Carbon dioxide is a major greenhouse gas that is produced by burning fossil fuels. When too much solar radiation is absorbed, the earth warms up, which alters climates around the world.

GREENHOUSE GAS

Any gas that is good at absorbing and retaining the sun's heat. Carbon dioxide, which is released into the atmosphere by the burning of fossil fuels, is a greenhouse gas. Greenhouse gasses contribute to a gradual warming of the earth, which is called the greenhouse effect.

RADIOACTIVITY

A stream of particles that emits from a source such as uranium. This energy can cause sickness or be fatal to the people who are exposed to the radiation.

RENEWABLE ENERGY

Any kind of energy where the source won't get used up. Solar power, waterpower, and wind power are examples of renewable energy.

Index